FICTIONS OF HIS LIFE

Pfano Mush

For information contact Pfano Mush on:

Email: mushpfano@gmail.com or

Twitter: @Pfano_mush

Note.

This anthology would not be on your palms if my Strength Provider Jesus was not reigning in my life.

Tlangelani Mashila, Thank you for editing the crappy mistakes I made in the manuscript. Working with me was not easy, but because we had a bigger goal in mind, you did not give up. I appreciate you.

Dear reader, I will forever be grateful for not only making me a few Rands richer, but for granting my work your time. I hope and pray that this book puts a smile on your face and ignites thoughts and conversations in the luxurious comfort of your precious mind.

Family and friends, I love you. Your continuous support builds me every single day. May our Savior add more days to the ones we'll spend together.

The Jailed Prisoner.

1

"don't get too comfortable, you'll be back Pastor-Bishop-whatever you call yourself," said Sergeant Pietersen as he gave Patrick his parole documents.

Patrick did not respond to what the Sergeant said to him because he thought that he would be disobeying what was written in the bible in the book of EPHESIANS 4:29. He tried by all means to ignore all negativity that was thrown at him. Most prisoners, that were saved, believed that he was a changed man and had confidence that he was ready to face the real world. But it was a different case with the jailers. They deduced that Patrick was going to be back in jail because there had never been a prisoner that was released and didn't go back to jail within a year.

Patrick was arrested for murder and attempted murder. He killed his wife after he caught her with another man in their bedroom. He plunged her all over her face with a spade and stabbed the man that he caught her with on his genitals and almost cut off his leg. He couldn't finish off the man because he miraculously escaped. After he had calmed down, he called the police and handed himself over. He only served 10years of the 25years sentence.

When he walked out of the main gate at prison, he paused for a minute to take in the fresh breeze and he briefly adjusted his ears to the noise of the small town. He didn't know how he felt at that moment but he was mesmerized by all that was before his eyes. The town was completely different, a lot had changed in just 10years.

While he was still trapped in the amusement, a taxi driver hooted at him.

"hey papa! Are you going or what?" shouted the taxi driver.

"oh yes, I'm coming." Said Patrick.

It only took 20minutes to get to his house but since it was a taxi, it took longer than that. The driver had to be dropping people and picking up people at different places and Patrick ended up arriving home an hour later.

"so this is it..." whispered Patrick while standing at the gate outside his house. It wasn't locked, so he opened it and walked towards the front door.

After knocking three times, Monica opened the door.

"hello my child," murmured Patrick.

"papa," said Monica wearingly.

She had no idea that her father was released. She hadn't seen him in ten years. When he was arrested, she was only 12 years old but she still remembered how he looked like. She didn't keep contact with him because her mother's family took her away and had forbidden her to see him as they were afraid of what they thought he would have done to her. She knew exactly what he had done to her mother but she had forgiven him.

She gazed at him for a while before she got out of the house to get a clear view of him as she thought she was hallucinating. After a few moments, she was convinced that it was him. She hugged him immediately. Patrick was shocked at her reaction. He didn't expect her to welcome him. He expected to be chased away since he killed her mother. But Monica was already over that.

''babe who's outside?'' Asked Monica's boyfriend, Lambani.

Lambani was living with Monica in the house. He moved in when Monica passed to grade 12 after she felt that it was time to move back to her parent's house. Her Aunt allowed her as she was already old enough. She asked him to move in because she was bored and needed help in Science. But that wasn't so much of a good idea. They were basically living as husband and wife, and she never got the help that she needed in Science. She got a 30% in her matric final exam results, and a higher certificate pass. She was a top achiever at school and was capable of getting a Bachelor's pass but Lambani kept her away from her studies which led to the poor results.

''Who's inside?'' Asked Patrick.

''uhm, my boyfriend.'' Answered Monica.

''He lives with you? In my house?'' Patrick asked as he was processing the news in his head.

''I'll tell him to move out,'' said Monica.

"you better tell him to move out, you can't be living together as husband and wife when you're not even married, the bible condemns it!" exclaimed Patrick.

"The bible condemns it? I'm sure that's not the only thing that the bible condemns. I heard it also condemns murder..." said Monica.

"Monica, look, I've changed." Murmured Patrick

"really? It's only your first day here and you want to control everything!" Shouted Monica.

"you're my daughter and I care for you," said Patrick

Lambani came out of the house after he heard the two shouting.

"what's going on?" Asked Lambani.

"this is my dad, Patrick, the man I told you about." Said Monica.

''oh the dude that killed your mom? Bra get outta here before I call the police,'' said Lambani as he tried to threaten Patrick.

''no, it's fine. He got released today. He's gonna be staying with us,'' said Monica.

Lambani did not like the moving in of Patrick although the house wasn't his. He knew that having Patrick in the house would mean that a lot of things would come to a halt. For instance, he would no longer throw parties in the house, his relationship with Monica would no longer be the same. He was intimidated, he couldn't throw him out because the house wasn't his. He tried to convince Monica to prevent him from living in the house by reminding her what he had done to her mother but Monica had missed her father, and she had forgiven him. She believed that he had changed and wanted to give him a chance.

2

Days went by, weeks passed, and Patrick was struggling to get a job. He tried all the supermarkets offering to work as a cleaner but failed, he tried the construction sites, public schools and hospitals and some had an open vacancy but they didn't want to hire a convicted criminal. Society was unforgiving to murderers. It was difficult for society to accept criminals back into the community after they were released, which made it difficult for them to have a fresh start and find jobs.

Things became a bit tense between Monica and her boyfriend Lambani. Lambani did not like Patrick, and Patrick also didn't like him. Lambani could see the hate and disgust in Patrick's eyes every time they were in the same room and that caused a lot of tension between him and Monica. He tried to deceive her into thinking that Patrick was still the same man so that she might throw him out but Monica persisted in her good thoughts about him. And that made Lambani angry, he couldn't stand not having control over Monica. In the past, Monica danced to his tune, he had her wrapped around his finger and it all changed when Patrick returned. He hated it!

So since Monica was out of his control, he decided to pick fights with her. He'd start arguments out of small issues and tried to link them to Patrick. He demanded things in the house, he shouted when he didn't like something and would get angry for no reason. Patrick couldn't get involved because he was told to back off by Monica.

One fateful day Lambani was just about to throw his tantrums and Monica was ready for him. Before he even went far, Monica asked him to pack his things and move out of the house. Lambani immediately cooled down and apologized. Monica didn't fall for it, she stood her ground and demanded that he moved out. Patrick was ecstatic! Seeing Lambani leave the house was a phenomenal moment to watch for Patrick. Before Lambani stepped out, Patrick made sure that he expressed his joy to Lambani. He told him that he had been praying and longing for that day ever since he got home, and that he served a mighty God and that was proof that his God does indeed exist. Lambani replied back by just saying it was not over and he would make sure that he sent him back to prison where he belonged, he made sure that it came out as a threat.

For once Patrick was at peace. He could see that Monica was heart-broken but knowing that Lambani was no longer in the house made all the difference.

Monica went through depression after Lambani left. She missed him and deep inside was regretting kicking him out. She called him every night to tell him that she loved him and how sorry she was, but Lambani did not believe that. He wanted her to choose between him and her Father but she couldn't do that.

Patrick was aware of their phone calls and he was disappointed. He wanted her to realize that Lambani wasn't good for her but that always led to a fight. So Patrick decided to let her do things her own way. But that didn't end well for both of them.

3

It only took one phone call to turn things around for Patrick. It was a Friday night when Lambani called Monica and asked her to meet at a fig tree in the Village. Patrick didn't want her to go out as it was already late but Monica insisted on going since Lambani had told her it was urgent. He let her go but his instincts told him something bad was about to happen. Before he followed her, he prayed and took a knife.

Monica arrived at the tree after a few minutes and found Lambani waiting for her. Without any hesitation, she asked what the problem was, but Lambani briefly took his time before answering her. In a low pitch, he spoke about how miserable her life was before she met him, the way he changed her and how happy they were before Patrick came into their lives.

Monica interrupted him while he was still talking and told him to get to the point, as she had no interest in listening to what he was saying. Lambani moved closer to her and asked her to repeat what she said, as she was about to, he punched her right on the face! He punched her as if she was one of the village boys. She fell down and he spat on her and kicked her shouting aggressively about how he had sacrificed his life for her. Patrick came out from where he was hiding and kicked him on the face.

He helped Monica get up and Lambani saw the knife that Patrick put in his back pocket. He got up and snatched it, but Patrick didn't let it go that easily because he knew that if he did, someone was going to get injured or in the worst case scenario, die. Monica shouted for help, the nearest house was just 500metres uphill and they could tell that someone was in trouble down there, so they called the police.

Patrick was still trying to take the knife but Lambani was just as strong as he was. Monica tried to interfere, she was pushing Lambani away but that actually gave him strength to get the knife and as soon as Patrick gained control of it, he jerked forward to stab Lambani but Monica came in the way. He stabbed her. The knife was deep in her throat, there was so much blood coming out. Monica dropped dead.

Lambani couldn't believe what had just happened. And he thought that Patrick would jump on him that instant and stab him, which he actually did after realizing his daughter was dead. Patrick made sure Lambani died painfully. He stabbed him thirty-five times on his chest. He was overtaken by anger.

The police arrived and they recognized Patrick. He was very famous for the crime he committed years ago. Killing his wife brutally was the worst thing that ever happened in that village. People started flocking in, they thought Patrick came back from jail just to kill Monica and they wanted to gang up on him and burn him but the police had already arrested him.

Few weeks later, Patrick pleaded guilty and the Magistrate sentenced him to life imprisonment.

RISE ABOVE.

The meatballs were perfectly done, all thanks to the recipe that I asked from my best friend Jeremiah who worked for the *Food Networks South Africa.* The Jasmine rice was almost done, I wasn't sure whether it was enough for the two of us because Noma always filled up her plate when I cooked it, and she never got tired of it. I couldn't make up my mind about which soup I should cook but since time was not on my side I decided to go for the *Cazuela* soup.

It was 19:30, I panicked as I carried the food to the dining room and the soup was still hot and that was good because she liked it warm. She was a few minutes from arriving and I hadn't taken a shower. I would have, I just didn't have enough time as I was doing chores all day. I had to turn the house upside down and lean it from top to bottom.

I took a shower immediately after setting the dining room. I only spent 2minutes in there, I rushed out, put on the cologne that she bought me, which was actually meant for special occasions but that night was her birthday so I had to. I wanted her to feel special as she knew that it was my favorite cologne and I only used it on special occasions. I thought it was going to be a great night, I planned well in advance and it seemed as if things were going to go smoothly as I had anticipated.

Before I went down stairs I made the bed, since I didn't have time in the morning. Suddenly, I heard loud music outside. Without a doubt, I knew it was her. She usually played loud music in her car whenever she was stressed. It was her way of releasing the stress and the neighbors complained. But she didn't care about them. She was a loose cannon.

Something struck my mind as I was walking downstairs. I thought I had forgotten to do something. The candles! I had forgotten to light the candles!

But it was too late because she was already in the kitchen and had a clear view of the dining room.

"*hey honey,*" as I kissed her on the cheek.

"*Hi, I miss you,*" she replied tiredly.

"*I miss you too, it was a long day without you, happy birthday,*" I said that while giving her the present that I was saving up for the past six months.

"*what's inside?*" she asked.

I could see the curiosity in her eyes and I had a feeling that she might not like what I bought her because she was a woman of class. I was lucky to have her as my wife. People didn't understand why she married me out of all the men, it was expected that she would marry one of the top executives at her father's company but she chose me. I was just a model who was struggling to get a breakthrough or a gig that would put my face out there. I was getting promotional gigs here and there but they weren't building up my profile.

After opening the wrapped box,

''seriously! Timberlands? You bought me a pair of boots for my 30th birthday?''

''honey you know that's what I can afford, I wanted to buy you a...uhm...a bracelet or a necklace, but you have lots of those.'' I anxiously tried to calm her down.

'' What am I supposed to do with your heavy, cowboy boots now?'' she said while she threw them down.

"*what were you expecting me to get you*?" I was perturbed.

" *A job, get a job Vusi!*'' She shouted.

I knew that trying to please her was never going to work. Every time I tried to do something for her she made sure that she reminded me that I did not have a job. She always cautioned me that I was nothing without her and that I was less of a man. Sometimes I would get beatings, she slapped me, kicked me, and she threw anything that was near her at me. I was frustrated because there were times when she made me feel special, subsequently she would make me feel like trash.

I pulled myself together and sucked up what she just said.

"*I'm sorry, can we at least have dinner?*" I said sorrowfully.

''*Let's see what you cooked,*'' She said while walking to the dining room.;

''what the hell is this?'' She said while holding the soup bowl.

''you don't like it?'' my heart pounded.

''there's nothing that you're good at, I don't even know why I fired my Chef.''

''Baby come on, don't do this, you've always loved my food.''

She splashed the soup all over my chest then spat on my face before going upstairs. I was overwhelmed. I couldn't believe, nor had I ever imagined that she would insult my cooking. If she got rid of her Chef, it clearly meant that she loved my cooking. I didn't know what was happening with her tonight.

As for splashing the soup on me, I was glad it wasn't as hot as it was when I put it on the dining table because if it was, I would've been admitted to the hospital for the second time for a similar incident.

Three months ago I spent two nights at a hospital after she splashed hot water on me while I was sleeping. I should've suffered third degree burns from this but I guess God's grace was sufficient enough. When I asked her why she had done it, she said that she wanted me to wake up and do my chores, she begged me not to report the case to the police and I didn't because she told me that she regretted it and she was sorry.

After reminiscing all that had occurred, I sat down and ate the food that we were supposed to eat together while celebrating her birthday. But things didn't go according to plan. I left some food for her just in case she changed her mind about not eating.

I woke up the following morning in the guestroom. I didn't sleep with Noma in our bedroom since I was too scared to sleep next to her because of what had happened the previous night. I stayed up to two hours from the time the incident happened, patiently waiting for her to come downstairs but she didn't. All that I heard was her laughter. She was on the phone. I wondered whom she was talking to at that time of the night since all her friends were married. I suspected that it was probably a man that she was talking to and it made perfect sense since we our marriage was on the rocks. But I doubted my thoughts.

I spent over an hour drowned in my own thoughts about the way Noma had been treating me and whether she was actually cheating on me. At the same time, I felt like a coward. I was frustrated about my own sexuality. Ten years ago, I was a happy man. I actually felt like a man in fact, I was a man, but at that present moment, I was bewildered. I regretted meeting Noma at that strip club. Actually I regret being a stripper. Because if I never took that job, I wouldn't have met this evil lady. I understand that she made me quit stripping and do something which was a bit useful like modeling, which was ironic because she had been giving me a lot of slack on that.

After sabotaging myself with maim thoughts, I walked over to the kitchen to make some breakfast. As usual, on the fridge there was a note that Noma pasted. It was a list of all the chores that I had to do. And that list was not as long as the previous one, she instructed me to just clean the house and change the sheets in our bedroom.

I realized that something was missing. She usually wrote, ''*Love Noma*,'' at the bottom of the list but on that one she didn't, within an instant I felt the thought of her cheating on me slowly approaching, but I shook it off or my attention was drawn to my ringing phone in the guestroom. I ran there as fast as I could, thinking that it might be Noma but graciously, it wasn't her. She didn't like it when I didn't answer her phone calls or replied to her texts immediately.

"Jeremiah, my man,"

"yeah, wassup?" greeted Jeremiah.

"I'm alright,"

"that's not convincing enough, I hope your wife isn't beating you up again."

Jeremiah was my best friend, we used to talk about everything and as awkward as it was, I confided in him. He tried very hard to persuade me to report the abuse to the police but because of the stigma around man abuse I couldn't. Another thing that stopped me was the fact that I didn't have a job. More reason was that if I had opened a case against Noma, I wouldn't have afforded the lawyers and Noma would have raged down on me with her army of advocates.

I told Jeremiah about what Noma had done to me and the gift that I bought her the previous night and he reacted the way that I thought he would. He couldn't contain the rage that he had towards Noma. I made him angry because I wasn't standing up to Noma neither was I agreeing to report the abuse to the police or to leave her. I couldn't leave her because I depended on her financially. And she had done so much for me.

At that moment I strongly felt that our friendship was all about the abuse. He had been changed from being *my guy, my main man*, into a nanny, a mother of a sixteen year old daughter or a therapist or some psychologist. I swore I felt like a baby whenever I spoke to him. Our conversations were just too awkward and too aggressive since he was trying to get me to open a case against Noma or simply stand up to her.

In conclusion to the phone call which was almost two hours, Jeremiah threatened to approach the police himself but he'd firstly pay Noma a visit. When I tried to warn him, he hung up.

I stressed the whole day while I was doing my chores, I was tempted to go to Noma's office but that would've pissed her off because she didn't want me near her working place or even having me in public spaces. She thought I was an embarrassment. She didn't say it to my face but actions speak louder than words.

Time passed by and I was patiently waiting for Noma but she wasn't showing up. When I tried her cell, it was off as was the case when I tried calling Jeremiah.

It was around ten o'clock at night that I heard the car parking in the garage. I was slumbering on the couch, what surprised me was that there was no loud music.

''you bastard!'' Noma slammed the door.

I knew instantly that Jeremiah paid Noma a visit. I braced myself before she came into the living room.

''where are you?'' she walked in with a bottle of beer.

It was pretty much clear that she was drunk. That year she had only gotten drunk when she lost a big contract to her biggest competitor, which didn't sit well with her and sort of led her to drinking.

''you're such an ass you know, I mean what kind of a man sends another man to stand up for him to his wife?'' she shouted as she was opening another bottle of beer.

"I didn't send him, he was just trying to help but I told him that our marriage was fine…"

''fine? Are you crazy? You don't have a job dude!''

''baby, I think you have had enough drinks for tonight, let's go upstairs.'' As I tried taking the bottle from her.

I thought she was giving in, and then *''clink!''* was the sound of the bottle that broke on my head. She hit me with a beer bottle. I was bleeding.

"I've had enough, this ends here, I am going to the police," I murmured while getting up.

She blustered to laughter as if I had told a joke.

"you can't even afford a lawyer honey,'' she whispered into my ears.

''no one's going to believe you.'' She laughed.

''they will!'' I cried out.

''Do you think that they would take an unemployed man with just a computer certificate seriously over a woman that holds an MBA and is an Executive at a multibillion rand company?'' She sarcastically questioned me.

But she made a great point.

After she uttered those words I lost all my strength, I didn't have the zeal to leave the house anymore but before I completely gave up, Jeremiah appeared from nowhere.

''stop it!' shouted Jeremiah as he put his phone in his pocket.''

''what the hell are you doing here?'' Noma anxiously exclaimed.

''you said there's no proof and I've got it all here, in my phone, I sent the video right now to the captain of JMPS...someone's going to jail.'' said Jeremiah.

STOP MAN-ABUSE

NAKISANI

1

The alarm went off at exactly 5:00 am and as usual, she pressed the snooze button before she was forced to wake up when it went off again. She was not, nor had she ever been a morning person. She walked to the bathroom to do her business as she fantasized about holiday days gone by and the adventures she went on.

The holidays had just come to an end which meant it was back to waking up early. During the holidays, Nakisani woke up at around 10 o'clock which explained why she was grumpy. She came out of the bathroom after 30minutes, which was a record for her since she usually too forever doing her business. It also took her another 30minutes to dress up, comb her hair, brush her school shoes and pack one book in her bag just in case she didn't receive any new books. It was common knowledge that on the first day of school, barely anything was done in class. She was determined that the New Year was going to see a new Naki.

''I told you that this tunic is the perfect fit, but you thought it was too big,'' said Vho-Mme as she joyfully

gazed at Nakisani eating her breakfast in the dining room.

All meals were to be eaten in the dining room, no food was allowed in the sitting room or in bedrooms because the furniture was driven all the way from Botswana from the Legendary furniture making company ''BROTHERS OF WOOD,'' so if the furniture was to be stained, it would cost a lot to get the stains removed because it could only be cleaned by the detergents that were sold at the company in Botswana and they were pretty expensive.

''*Grade 11! I was told it's not an easy grade but I'm sure and I know that you my girl, will definitely make it through with distinctions!*'' said Pastor N.

''*Of course dad, I never disappoint, do I?*'' Asked Nakisani pensively.

''*you've never disappointed me my darling*,' said Pastor N.

''*My girl, this year you really have to get those totals you were aiming for, I'm tired of seeing 99's*,'' an enthusiastic Vho-Mme exclaimed.

"Ok! I get it people! May I leave now before Fhatu complains? We don't wanna be stuck in the traffic!" shouted Nakisani as she ran out of the house.

That was basically how Nakisani's whole life had been. She had been tortured by the talks her parents gave her every single morning, not a day went by without someone reminding her that she has to work very hard because the world was watching and the church had high expectations from her. But she never let the pressure get to her because she was always the best at everything she did.

Her intelligence was immeasurable. Nakisani was the full package, she was one of the most beautiful girls in Venda. She had a perfect body and was toned from the exercises she got from the various sports she played and she was a great leader both in the community as well as her school. She was the "IT GIRL" and was confident with her place in society.

2

Joy was visible amongst learners, everyone was chatting about the adventures they all went on during the holidays. Everyone was positive about the New Year, mostly the grade 12's since it's their final school year. It seemed as if most learners could not find their friends because the whole school was mixed up with new learners & new parents trying to find their way.

Two learners who could not find their bestie were Rinae & Ashley, not because she got lost in the crowd but because she hadn't arrived yet and they didn't know.

"Dude, are you sure you texted her this morning?" asked Rinae.

"Yes man, I texted her right after the video call, you know how Naki is, she loves making 'fabulous entrances' she might land here in a chopper or something" said Ashley.

"Hey guys!" Shouted a jovial Nakisani.

The look on Rinae's & Ashley's face was invaluable! They were so ecstatic when they heard Naki's voice. They hadn't seen her in a long since Naki went on vacation with her family at the heart of Zambia in one the best resorts in Africa.

Siren

There was no assembly at the school hall because one of the staff members had lost the keys to the hall and the spare keys were nowhere to be found, so everyone blissfully walked to their respective classes.

Grade 11A, that's her class. It's labelled 'A' for a very good reason, it represents the Top 40 learners of the grade & Nakisani occupied position 1. Rinae and Ashley are 2 & 3 respectively. So the triplets are the most academically intelligent and most envied in the school.

Siren

Right after the siren, Mrs. Booi walked into 11A, and the young boys could not control themselves, they showed how exhilarated they were by Mrs. Booi's beauty, her curvaceous hips, her long hair, and her sexy light-skinned legs. The woman is beautiful, all heads turn when she passes by, many are shocked when they find out that she's married with three children and she still has a body to die for.

''*morning class,*'' said Mrs. Booi.

''*morning ma'am*,'' replied the leaners.

''*welcome back from the holiday, I am Mrs. Booi I will be teaching you Physical Science, Chemistry Section. I believe we haven't prayed, right*?'' enquired Mrs. Booi.

''*Yes!*'' shouted the learners.

"*okay, Nakisani my girl, could please start up a song before we pray*?'' requested Mrs. Booi.

Nakisani was a well-known learner in the school. Her activeness gained her popularity amongst the educators, learners and even the maintenance staff. Hence Mrs. Booi pointed her out so quickly.

Nakisani then sang one of her favorite gospel songs, ''*Ke Na Le Modisa*''

The whole class backed her up and after they were done singing Mrs. Booi read a scripture from the bible and gave them some motivation and encouragement for the year then she prayed.

Right after the prayer a boy walked in. An incredibly handsome one, there were a lot of handsome boys in that school but that one was just strikingly gorgeous. His skin was beautifully spotless, he had angelic brown eyes, his tantalizing lips had every girl drooling, he was not too tall nor too short just the average height, he had a bit of fuzz on the chin which made him look more masculine. Quite a beautiful boy.

There was a moment of silence when he stepped in, all eyes were glued onto him, and the attention was too overwhelming he couldn't keep his head up.

''May I help you?'' asked Mrs. Booi

''yes, I'm new. Is this grade11A?'' asked the new learner.

''ma'am he is my friend from home, his name is Dylan. Come sit this side Dylan'' said Chris while showing Dylan where to sit.

"no, wait, did the administrator tell you to come to this class?'' enquired Mrs. Booi.

"yes, she said my grade10 final report marks qualify for this class,''

"alright, no problem. Welcome to our little family.'' Said Mrs. Booi with the most genuine smile.

Dylan walked to the back of the class to sit with his homeboy. Chris was naughty. He happened to be one of the boys who hit on Mrs. Booi the previous year when she just arrived as a new teacher. This got him into a lot of trouble, so much that he was almost expelled. What saved him from expulsion is his competency. He had won awards on behalf of the school in Sports and Physics competitions and he was one of the top 40 learners.

Ashley couldn't control herself, she literally turned her chair to face backwards just to stare at Dylan. She was quite a character and had a fascinating personality. She had done all unimaginable things all in the name of "YOLO." She also had a fear of missing out. She influenced Naki and Rinae to do things which would land them into trouble. But they'd never been into any trouble since they always found a way out.

Nakisani on the other hand kept things together by pretending as if she did not notice Dylan. She didn't want to show how impressed she was although she despised how Ashley was staring at Dylan. She thought she was embarrassing herself. Rinae was chatting to some girl about the Glee club and the plans that their leader, Nakisani had for the year.

Pastor Ndou together with his wife Vho-Mme led the biggest congregation in the country. They had been in the ministry for 21 years and they changed the lives of many people. They received awards from various institutions for the community service that they did in villages across the country. Pastor N, was not only a Preacher of the Gospel of God, he was also a renowned businessman and bestselling Author. He owned an orchard which supplied fruits to various supermarkets in the country. Over the past 10 years he has written 12 books of which, 7 became the bestsellers in the country. He also had a slot on one of radio stations, where he motivated listeners and gave marriage counselling. He was the chairperson of SACL (South African Christian Leaders) amongst many leadership roles.

Vho-Mme directed the management of the church since Pastor Ndou was always preoccupied. Vho-Mme was gifted in counselling, that was her area of specialization. Many marriages would have been broken if it wasn't for her. On Sundays she conducted the orchestra while Nakisani led the worship team.

They were labelled the "power couple" by *Forces* Africa magazine. They used their influence in society to make more money but at the same time they ensured that they brought change to the lives of people.

But then there was a place where they were misusing their power. On Nakisani. She was a bright girl, brilliant at school, had the voice of an angel, and gifted in various ways, it seemed as if she loved her life, and pleased with everything around her but that was not how it actually was. She was dying on the inside. Her parents continuously commanded her to do what they thought should be done, they put her in a leadership position at church when she was only 14years old. The worship team had over 30 singers and all of them were adults! And they expected her to be leading people that were old enough to be her parents.

Apart from controlling her at that current phase, they also had a future planned for her. They told her that she was going to be a Doctor, and she will study medicine in Pretoria, as it is close enough to Venda. They even went as far as planning her marriage, although they were rich and successful, they still had strong cultural and traditional views on things such as marriage. They wanted her to get married at the age of 26, and they were still deciding on who will have Nakisani's hand in marriage between the Mbedzi's son and the Nxumalo's son. A close relative once called them dictators and they got so angry. They were supporting the relative financially but after the remark she made, they cut her off.

But Nakisani is accustomed to her parent's reign. She was living life knowing that everything was planned for her. She didn't think of going against her parents, standing up for herself, or letting them know that she was numb on the inside. She thought that if she ever went against them, the world would automatically turn against her. It literally would, because she was everything that people expected her to be and if she was to change a single thing or to be the total opposite, she would experience her own type of world war.

<u>4</u>

Nakisani's school knocked out at *14:15* and as usual the trio walked out of the class together.

''it's only the first day and that Dylan is getting all the attention,' whined Rinae.

''of course, it's no surprise to me, I mean, look at him. What do you think Naki?'' Asked Ashley.

''yeah he's good-looking,'' mumbled Naki.

Nakisani was turning 16 that year and she hadn't kissed a boy. Something which was very rare amongst her peers, girls in her class talked about boys and they had been dating since puberty kicked in, some had had sex more than a married couple. There were only a few girls in her class that kept their minds and bodies as *Temples of God*.

But Nakisani had her moments, there were times when she let it all out. She talked to Ashley about *''girls stuff*.''

''my driver is already here, see you tomorrow,'' said Naki as she hugged Rinae and Ashley.

''okay don't forget the auditions pamphlet,'' shouted Rinae.

The auditions pamphlet that Rinae was taking about was for the *Glee Club*. The Glee Club was founded by Nakisani. Rinae and Ashley helped Nakisani run the Glee Club. They had auditions every year on the second week of the first term. Nakisani was the Executive Producer, while Rinae and Ashley were the Co-directors. The club gained popularity after its first performance, they performed once every term for the learners and at all parent's meetings. Nakisani was always the star of every show, not only because she was the founder of the club but because there was no one who could have done it better than her and the fans loved her, they never got tired of her.

Fhatu was Nakisani's assigned driver. He was the only person who worked for the Ndou family who did not expect Nakisani to be the *''Golden child,''* he did not expect her to be a sweet, grounded, humbled, pastor's-kid. He wanted her to just be what she wanted, he wanted her to behave like other teenage girls, and he expected her to be naughty and rebellious. Which was exactly what happened when Naki was with him. She confided in Fhatu when she was going through rough patches. Fhatu was always there to listen to her and to give her advice whenever necessary.

She got in the *Merc AMG* SUV. It was registered "Nakisani 01," and there were others parked at home. When Fhatu asked about how the first day of school was, Nakisani didn't waste any time.

She began taking about Dylan, she confessed to Fhatu about how she liked him, and she had never felt that way about a boy. Fhatu was happy that Nakisani finally had a crush on a boy because he was beginning to think that she was not straight, which would have been a catastrophe.

"ah brah yanga, ndo hangwa uni vhudza uri nga matsheloni hopfi mini weh," said Naki. (My guy, I forgot to tell you what they said in the morning)

"khai ambe ripfe," replied Fhatu. (Talk, I'm listening).

"eh namusi hopfi eh, habe grade11 I a konda nahone ndi khou tea u to vhala nduri ndo tou di funga nyana so, ari tsha toda u vhona zwi 99 hezwila zwe navha ni tshi zwi wana mahola," said Naki. (They said I have to study seriously, in fact we don't want to see the 99s that I used to get last year).

"lol ai vha tshantsa, vha khou nyaga atshi tou wana 100?" asked Fhatu. (They're crazy, so they want you to get 100?)

'Yes! They actually are expecting me to get totals man" shouts Naki.

''Mara it's not something bad, it's for your future,'' said Fhatu

''future? What future? The future that you are talking about is the one that they planned for me,'' exclaimed an annoyed Naki.

Fhatu's phone rang later on, it was Pastor N's P.A (Gloria). She was telling him to take Nakisani to church after she had freshened up.

She was going to be interviewed by a TV host about how being a ''P.K'' (pastor's kid) was like and the challenges she met. She could have used the platform to tell the world and her parents that she was sick of being treated like property and tired of living up to people's very, very high expectations but she kept it together and pretended like she loved every moment of her life and lied to the TV viewers by saying that she felt really humbled to be part of a family that served the Lord with multitudes of people.

Toward the end of the interview Naki was asked to sing and she sang one of her grandmother's favorite hymns ''blessed assurance.'' She told the interviewer that her grandmother loved the song so much that she used to sing it to her every day in her early childhood years when she went to bed. And her grandmother told her that nothing would please her more if Naki would sing the very same song at her funeral service. The previous year her grandmother died peacefully in her sleep, and Naki kept the promise. She sang at her grandmother's funeral service.

After the interview, her mom was obviously overexcited that her baby girl was on TV, Pastor N couldn't make it in time because he had an important business meeting but he watched the show when he got home.

Just when she thought it was enough for the day, the Evangelist arrived. Evangelist Tshilongamulenzhe, he was the right-hand man, the number one follower of Pastor N and their friendship had grown beyond being church leaders, Evangelist was a part of the Ndou family. Nothing happened without his knowledge and consent.

But Nakisani did not like him because he was the driving force behind the control that her parents had over her, every time Naki won her parent's favour over something, Evangelist T got involved and changed their minds. He never wanted Nakisani to have things done her way, he was always there when decisions were to be taken.

The same evening Evangelist T arrived at the Ndou residence to obviously give his thoughts about the TV interview but as soon as he walked in the living room, Nakisani greeted him then walked out because she knew that he was there to comment on the interview and would definitely find something to criticize. Naki saved herself from the annoying Evangelist by heading straight to bed.

5

Chris spent the night at Dylan's house because Dylan's mom (Catherine) was working late.

"dude, do you recognize that chick that was on TV?" asked Chris.

"yeh, that chick is hot man! I kept starring at her, like I couldn't focus! If only I had known that Venda had pretty girls like her... I would've came back sooner," said an amused Dylan.

"and she can sing!" exclaimed Chris.

"yes! That's how I'm gonna get close to her, I have to join that Glee club that she spoke about on the TV interview," said an enthusiastic Dylan.

"seriously dude? Are you ever gonna forget about this music thing?" asked Chris ruggedly.

Dylan had been musical since he was a child. He learnt how to sing and play all music instruments through his dad (Justin M) before his mom divorced him.

His dad was a music sensation in South Africa and he was the best-selling artist in the country, with that, came a lot of fame, which got to his head. He cheated on Catherine and she found out from the Sunday papers. That led to their divorce. But most people did not know Dylan as his mother kept him away from the public eye.

"hey boys!" Shouted Catherine as she took off her stilettos before throwing herself on her lazy-chair.

"hey mom!" said Dylan

"how was school my boy?"

"it was fine, except being freaked out by the stares I got from the girls, and then there was this beautiful one who was on TV a couple of minutes ago, Nakisani... I thought I had seen all beauty till today," said an amused Dylan.

Catherine was a progressive mom. She wanted Dylan to be comfortable around her because she was all that Dylan had. He didn't have a full time father so she tried to be the best parent. One of the things that she had to do was to talk about girls with Dylan, and he was always comfortable and frank with her.

"okay ah, I'll be leaving now neh, it's getting late" said Chris as he was leaving.

"okay boy boy, see you tomorrow," said Dylan as he walked Chris out.

<u>6</u>

Dylan woke up early the following day, his mind, like a caged rat, was running around all the possibilities that might occur when he approaches Nakisani.

He rehearsed what he was going to say before the mirror. He did that before and after he took a shower. He made sure his uniform was neatly ironed, his shoes were shining and brushed his very short hair and the moustache that was growing slowly. After he was satisfied with what the mirror showed him, he went to the dining room to get some breakfast. Vho-Macy, his house keeper, arrived early enough to make him and Catherine breakfast.

Before he was done eating, his mom started the car,

''eish mom seriously? I'm not even done with breakfast,'' he spoke as if she could hear him.

He ran to his room, grabbed his schoolbag and the heavy physics text book that every learner didn't like to carry.

It was a ten minutes' drive from Dylan's house to school but it only took that long when Catherine was not speeding. She had been slammed with three speeding tickets the previous year. They warned her that if she was to get another ticket, they would lock her up.

"bye, see you later tonight," said Dylan as he got off the car.

He ran to the school hall for assembly because the siren went off a long time ago. He suddenly became anxious because he kept thinking about what he was going to say to Nakisani and he didn't know how she would react.

On the top of his list, he wanted to tell her that she looked beautiful on TV the previous night but he was again, unsure about the way that she would react. His mind kept running in those thoughts from the time he met Chris on the way to the hall, he wasn't even vigilant when the principal was talking at the assembly. He only became attentive when he walked into the class and he saw Nakisani standing with a group of girls from the B class who were talking about how amazing she was on TV.

"just go ask to talk to her dude," said Chris as he tried to persuade him.

Finally he made up his mind and approached her.

"hi, I am Dylan," as he trembles,

"oh hey," replied Naki with a smile.

Dylan then asked her to talk in private, Naki didn't even hesitate. She dispensed herself from the crowd and followed Dylan to his desk. Dylan began by telling her that he watched the show and he really enjoyed watching it, Nakisani tinted while trying not to grin too much. Dylan could not stop smiling. As the conversation went on, Dylan's nerves came down and Nakisani stopped with the blushing. They became comfortable.

They had moved from talking about the TV interview to Dylan's old school and why he left. Ashley starred at them as they talked and she felt proud as a friend, she had never seen Nakisani being so indulged in a conversation with a guy, Nakisani had never talked to a guy for more than 15minutes, and in fact she always looked at guys deep in their eyes when they spoke to her, she did that as a form of intimidation and it always worked.

But with Dylan it was different, she barely looked at him. Dylan on the other hand, kept looking at Chris and checked if the teacher had arrived. Chris was giving him signals that he was doing great!

''*so I heard you say that you want to be a Doctor*,'' said Dylan.

''*yes, I want to be a doctor*,'' replied Naki as she rolled her eyes, knowing that he's going to start questioning her about the decision.

''*but why? Ah, look, imagine Beyoncé working in a hospital*.'' Laughed Dylan.

''*excuse me?*''

''*Nakisani you have a very beautiful voice, are you seriously going to waste your time by going to study medicine? And the rest of your life saving people's lives, in a hospital. Rather use your voice to change someone's life*.''

Siren.

The first period commenced then Nakisani used that as an excuse to end the conversation. She didn't want to tell Dylan that medicine was chosen for her by her parents.

<u>7</u>

Siren. (Break time)

''So, what was Dylan saying?'' asked Ashley as she munched the left over pizza from her house.

''we were talking about the TV interview, may I taste your pizza?'' replied Naki as she tried to change the topic.

She did not want to talk about Dylan since she knew that if she talked about him she would be giving Ashley and Rinae the chance to ask questions and she would be compelled to answer honestly as she never lied to her friends.

''oh-oh, speak of the devil,'' said Rinae while he was putting away his lunchbox preparing to leave.

''this guy is really into you! You better not shut him out!'' said Ashley as she followed Rinae.

Dylan sat at the edge of the bench. Nakisani remained stationed on the bench and tried to eat her fruit salad in pleasure.

"So you haven't answered my question about your career choice," said Dylan.

Naki then looked away trying to figure out what answer she could give him because she didn't want to tell a stranger that she didn't choose her own career as it was too personal. And if she was honest with Dylan she would've tainted her parent's reputation because they forced her to take medicine as her career choice.

She could not think of anything else to say, her gut gave her a feeling to tell the truth but at the same time she would be betraying her mom and dad until she looked into Dylan's eyes and got lost in the moment.

"Nakisani? Hello?" while waving his hand.

She finally said that she loved medicine, she loved helping people and she wants to make a difference in the lives of her community members. Dylan was disappointed.

He asked her if she ever considered doing music and she said yes, she loved music and would love to do it professionally someday, that would be after she got her degree.

So they began talking about their music experiences, Nakisani told him about the praise team that she led at church and Dylan obviously told her that his dad was a music star. Nakisani was quite captivated when Dylan was talking about his dad.

After talking about music, Nakisani asked Dylan to sing her a song. Dylan refused at first but he couldn't resist the sad look that Naki gave him while he was whining. He decided to sing her a song titled, *"TITANIUM."* Nakisani then joined in later in the song.

Siren.

"that was nice," said Nakisani

"yeah, you have a beautiful voice," when his eyes were stuck to Nakisani's.

"we have to get to class, the siren..."

"yeah, I know,"

They head to class.

8

Pastor N decided to take some time off work so he could have quality time with his wife. He had not been around for some time.

''Honey, you know I'm so proud of our little angel Nakisani, she is so beautiful, she is talented, she is a top learner at school, It makes me feel so proud,'' gushed Vho-Mme.

''The Lord has really blessed us, she is one of a kind. That is why she must get married to one of the highly respected families, either the Mbedzi's or the Nxumalo's.'' said Pastor N.

They continued to talk about the plans that they had for Nakisani and it got them excited, they spoke as if all their plans would come to pass. They had so much faith in the future ahead, little did they know that Nakisani was going to turn against them.

''but one problem that I have is the fact that she loves music too much,'' groaned Pastor N.

''ah vha songo dinalea (don't worry), she will never do music, she will only sing at church...Eish! You know I

forgot to tell you that some record label owner called "Freddy" asked to sign Nakisani on his label because he thinks Nakisani will be a great gospel artist,'' whimpered Vho-Mme.

''And that's never going to happen, I don't want my daughter to end up like those poor Gospel artists!'' shouted Pastor N.

9

When school knocked out, Dylan took a taxi to town to visit his friend (Freddy) a record label owner. He told him that wanted to record an album. He had been waiting his whole life for the opportunity. He wasn't allowed previously because they thought he was too young.

''so you want to make money like your dad neh,'' joked Freddy.

''no, I just love doing music, I have no money on my mind,'' Dylan calmly replied.

Freddy took out the contract and explained everything that Dylan was not going to comprehend by himself. He made sure that Dylan knew what he was getting himself into since Freddy had signed artists that pulled out when things became difficult and it cost him a lot of money. Immediately after signing the contract, he sang *"MONEY ON MY MIND."*

''you remind me of your dad,'' said an astonished Freddy.

Freddy worked closely with Justin M for a number of years and they had great passion for music which took them far until they decided to part ways. Freddy was tired of the spotlight and wanted to work behind the scenes as a producer while Justin M just wanted to perform and he never got tired of the spotlight, hence they decided to go separate ways. So he was not entirely surprised by the passion that Dylan had for music.

"Hey Freddy, I met this other chick at school and I was singing with her today, I know you've worked with a lot of talented artists but this one is just different man," said Dylan showing great excitement.

"Okay, bring her in studio, and we'll see what she got," said Freddy.

''okay I got to go now, I'll give my mom the contract so she can also sign it.''

''Sure thing boy, boy.'' said Freddy as he escorted him out.

Dylan was ecstatic when Freddy said that he could bring in Nakisani. He badly wanted to record a song with her. He wanted a song that would tell her how he felt about her. As he fantasized about the duet, he became excited, he couldn't think of anything else when he was going home, he even took out his notebook and pen, to make some adjustments to the lyrics that he had written the previous night.

When his mom got home, he immediately ran to her and told her about the song that he sang to Nakisani at school. He also told her that he felt different when he was with Nakisani and that he had heard many girls sing and he never connected with any of them.

After telling her about "the amazing Nakisani," he gave her the contract to sign. She looked at it and read through it carefully. She made sure that Dylan understood every section of the contract although Freddy had already done that. She didn't want Dylan to get himself into something that he would regret later in life. Catherine was a cautious mother because Justin M had signed a lot of contracts when they were still married and it caused a lot of conflicts and he was even sued for not complying with the terms of one of the contracts that he had signed.

10

Siren (Break time).

"hey," smiled Dylan.

"hey, how are you?" replied Nakisani.

"I'm fine and you?"

"I'm alright,"

Dylan then told Nakisani about the contract that he signed the previous day. Nakisani was so happy when Dylan told her that he was going to record an album. Dylan also mentioned that he wished he could record the song that they sang the other day. Nakisani's facial expression showed no interest, Dylan quickly noticed and changed the topic to Freddy's studio.

As he was talking about the studio, Nakisani kept looking at her watch. She only did that when she was trying to escape from a conversation, it always gave people the impression that she was rushing off somewhere, at that time she was trembling because she was scared of walking away from Dylan since she liked him. But she hated what Dylan was talking about. Her gut told her that he wanted to record a song with her and just when she thought maybe her gut is wrong Dylan said,

"How about we record a song together, an RnB song that I wrote myself,"

"I can't be caught dead singing any music that's not Gospel," murmured Nakisani.

"come on it's just a song," as Dylan tried to persuade her.

"My parents would kill me if they ever find out," Nakisani said uneasily.

"ah, okay, how about we record the song, and not release it until you feel it's the right time to release it," said Dylan.

"But what's the point of recording the song?" enquired Nakisani.

"You'll understand when we record the song...Please Nakisani," begged Dylan.

"You promise not to release the song?" Asked Naki.

"I promise Naki," said Dylan

"okay, when should I come?"

When Nakisani uttered those words Dylan jumped into the air and screamed,

"yes!"

He was really excited, he almost hugged her, but put himself together. Nakisani on the other hand was worried, she was not feeling good about the recording of the song, an RnB song for that matter. If Dylan ever released the song without her permission, she was going to freak out and she was going to be in trouble.

11

So the day finally arrived, Nakisani was in studio on time, she was given the lyrics, she went through them and the first thing she said after reading the lyrics was,

"You're a good writer, but you cannot expect me to record such erotic stuff, my parents would kill me.''

Dylan's heart pounded when she said that, he tried to explain to her as she was already picking up her bag as she wanted to leave. He told her that the song meant a lot to him and it was about a girl that he loved so much and he was too afraid to tell her because she might not give him the chance as she was from a well-known family and she would not want to taint her family name.

When he said that looking into her eyes, Nakisani immediately knew that he was talking about her. So she put her bag down and asked to listen to the beats of the song. After listening to the beats, she decided to stay. They recorded the song. Freddy was impressed as many artists that he had worked with usually took weeks to record a good song, but Nakisani and Dylan only took three hours.

After recording, Dylan told Freddy to keep the song in studio, not to release it until they had agreed to do so.

"thanks," said Dylan.

She winked at him, and smiled. She enjoyed recording the song, she loved the way Dylan was singing. He sang in an arousing way and when she looked at him he winked at her. It made her feel so special. She loved what she was looking at, she loved the way his lips moved and when he tried to rap.

Before she left the studio she reaffirmed him that if he released the song her life would be ruined. Dylan told her once more that the song was in good hands, and it would not be released unless she said so.

As they were going out, they decided to get some milkshakes at a nearby fast-food restaurant. They were just cooling off and talking about other things besides music.

Dylan asked her what she was really passionate about and he demanded an honest answer, Naki kept quiet for a minute before answering, she looked at him, grabbed her milkshake, took a sip, and then she looked back at him,

"music" she said, "I'm passionate about music, I love music and I do not imagine myself doing anything else other than that, music lives in me, not a day goes by without thinking or doing something that is connected to music, that is why I started that Glee Club at school.''

Dylan continued to ask her why she did not want to be an artist and she still did not want to tell him the truth but she felt that she had to tell him because he seemed like he was worth it.

She told him that she was not in charge of her own life, she had to get approval from her parents whenever she wanted to do something. She continued to tell him that she did not even choose a career for herself, and she let it all out! She told him that her parents are control freaks! She also warned him that if they found her with him at that restaurant, they were going to deal with him in some way.

After listening to the sad story life of Nakisani, Dylan told her that it is important that one must follow their passion, to do what they love, because if they do not, they will not succeed in anything. He lectured her about the importance of practicing your passion. And he also told her that no matter what, he will make sure that she followed her passion, even if it meant approaching her parents.

As they were talking they ordered more milkshakes, chocolate flavored ones. Nakisani told him everything, she almost cried. When Dylan noticed that she was about to cry he sang one of his songs, *"LET ME HOLD YOU DOWN."*

She felt so much better after Dylan sang. Later on, Fhatu walked in to tell her that she had a church practice to get to and she was already late. She immediately left the restaurant. Dylan felt good about what happened the whole day because he got to record a song with the girl that he loved and on top of that he got to take her out for drinks, he was a happy man.

ZWELAKHE

Bloody Sotho's! They think they own this place! Telling me that I'm wasting water as if I don't pay rent. We're all tenants here! In fact my rent is much higher than theirs!

I should've stabbed Lerumo with the knife that was on the table when he attacked me. Bustard! I knew he wouldn't pay back my money! I knew it, I just felt that he wouldn't pay me back but I fell for his sweet deceiving talk. I'm so stupid! I'm never trusting anyone in this house.

That fight could've ended badly if his friends didn't interfere, he thought he could beat me up like I was some bitch? No, no, I'm from Zululand, Zulu-men are warrior's, we're not Chickens like the Sotho's!

I woke up tired and depressed the following day. I had never felt so much wiriness in my life. It wasn't caused last night's fight, I was just going through a rough patch. I thought 2017 was going to be a great year for me but I felt as if I was actually going to die.

Things started falling apart when I met an Old lady in a taxi. I was coming from my part-time job in Kempton Park. I got in the first taxi that was heading to Sandton. I didn't talk to anyone in the taxi, there were only two guys and the Old lady. After a few minutes, I felt the old lady's gaze.

I ignored her. I thought she was just stunned by my dreadlocks. Everyone that had eyesight couldn't ignore my dreadlocks. They were reddish in colour, and when I was walking under the sun they looked purple. But they were also curly. After a few more minutes, she finally said something. She spoke in IsiXhosa. I understood a few Xhosa words. And as I had anticipated, she was staring at my dreads. I wasn't pleased at all because the first thing she said to me was to cut them off otherwise bad things would happen.

I thought she was crazy, probably drunk or she had been smoking weed or something, and if she was smoking weed then it was bad weed, I thought to myself, maybe I would hook her up with *Cacioppo*, the guy that sells the best weed in Jozi.

But to my surprise, she was actually a psychic, or Prophetess, I don't know the difference. She told me that she wasn't crazy, drunk, nor had she smoked weed. I wasn't easily impressed. I said nothing to her, I ignored her in the hoping that she would shut up. She didn't give up. She continued to say that if I kept ignoring her, things are going to get uglier. I looked at her and shouted, ''*Voetsek*! *Mthakathi*!''

I told her to back off! But that was the mistake that changed my life.

She started saying things. She prophesied. She revealed all my secrets, while she cursed me, not in detail but a series of events that were to occur. For starters, she gave me a flashback of what had happened at work that day. To be more precise, she reminded me of what happened at twelve o'clock in the Male toilets. I was having sex with a girl.

Old "Prophetess" continued to say that I was infected with an STD since the condom that I used was pricked. I began to shiver. The other two guys stopped the taxi and got out because they were freaked out. She continued to tell me that I was going to lose everything. I asked her how but she said she cannot disclose it to me as I was disrespectful to her. I had to prepare going back home although I don't like being home but I had to because a close family member was going to die. She said the family member was HIV positive and he had raped two of my cousins and they were infected as well. As if that was enough prophesy for one night, she added that my parents are going to encounter financial problems which will affect my studies at *College of Sandton*. Before she finished, she specified all the modules that I was going to fail. The Advertising module was one of them and to my surprise English studies made the list.

She did however give me one solution to some of my problems. She said I should cut my hair. Apparently my dreads were cursed by the person whom I got them from. I didn't believe her because I got the dreads from my aunt who was a Pastor. She cut her dreads because she felt that she had to look more like a Pastor. So it didn't make any sense to me. Once more, I told her to leave me alone, "*Voetsek*! *Wena Mthakathi*!"

I got out of the taxi feeling dizzy and nauseated. As I was walking, my mind was caged in what the Old lady said. I wasn't fully conscience until I was slapped.

The guy that hit me was enormous and scary. I could tell that I was going to be robbed as I tried to move, I noticed that there were three more men behind me. I lost all my strength. They took my wallet which had R500, my bank cards, ID card, Driver's license and student card. When they left, the Old lady's words reflected on my mind,

"*you will lose everything...*"

And I knew that was just the beginning.

I couldn't tell whether the robbery was just a random one or the Old Lady's curse had begun. But I almost felt as if the curse had started to take its course because my father was a Sangoma and he believed that witchcraft was real.

My father was a Sangoma for 30years. He performed magic in the village. One of the biggest things he had done, which was referred to as a miracle, was doing what Jesus did. He turned water into wine. And just when people thought they've seen it all, he made it rain for fourteen days nonstop. When people were sick he would heal their sickness, he opened wombs that were closed, he was the savior of the village. But if anyone had done him wrong, he would strike lightning on that person, literally. My childhood years were filled with miracles and witchcraft, but my father always told me that no one would ever curse me or bewitch me because I'm his son.

So I walked home from where the incident occurred, I wasn't conscience at all, my mind was still processing what had happened. I couldn't believe that it happened to me, my father was a powerful man spiritually, surely one of his 'spirits' could have protected me but that didn't happen. Maybe I no longer had the protection that my father had over me and I strongly believed that was caused by his transgression to the Christian religion. He joined one of the local churches in the village and within three months he was made the assistant pastor. Ridiculous! How does a Sangoma become a pastor? I however thought that my father was probably on a mission to demonize the whole church so he could have more followers in his craft.

I got home and found one of my housemates Nobuhle, in her night dress sitting on the Kitchen table. I tried to ignore her because she was an attention seeker. She noticed that I looked depressed and asked what the problem was, I told her that it was nothing then got into my room but she wasn't buying it. She barged in and closed the door. I told her to leave but she refused, she wanted to know what was going on.

I kept quiet for a moment. I gazed at her from her legs to her gorgeous face. She had beautiful light skin, extremely flawless! She didn't have a bra on and her night dress was so short and a bit transparent. I guessed that she had no panties on. I didn't really like her but she looked sexy that night, I was turned on.

I walked towards her, held her waist, and we kissed. Her lips were soft and she kissed me passionately. She held on to my shoulders and jumped to cross her legs around my waist. That was my favourite position. She grabbed my dreads and pulled them. I stopped kissing her. She asked me what was wrong, I stared at her, the thought of what the old lady said about my dreads was on my mind. I then asked her to leave, without any hesitation, she left the room.

I felt like a jerk. I had never rejected sex in my life. I then came to the realization that I was cursed. Hours and hours passed while I thought and tried to comprehend all the events that occurred that day until I broke down and cried myself to sleep.

I woke up the following morning feeling a bit better but I had to pee. So I went to the bathroom and as I was getting on with my peeing agenda, my morning was ruined. At first the color of my urine was black, a few seconds later it was blue then purple and finally the normal yellow color. I was shocked to the core and was officially convinced that the Old lady was indeed a real witch. I stood still and stared inside the toilet.

I couldn't flush and get out until someone knocked. I was stressed, irritated and angry at myself. I didn't know what was next, was I going to start breathing out smoke? Was I going to release white faeces? I became paranoid.

After being numb for a few hours I decided to take a shower. I wanted to see a doctor because I couldn't help having too many questions without any answers. While I was in the shower I felt a sudden sensation inside my bladder. It stopped for a moment. It began again, I turned off the water as I anticipated what was about to happen. It got painful but nothing that I couldn't handle, deep inside I knew it was one of the many things that the Old lady promised were going to happen.

And there it was, it came out, it was a worm. A big red worm came out of my bladder! Followed by blood. The blood didn't stop coming out, it was like water coming out of a tap and I was in so much pain, I fell down, and shouted for help. I knew there was no one in the house but surprisingly Lerumo came to my rescue. He was freaked out because there was so much blood. He carried me to his car and put a towel over me but once we were in the car the blood stopped. I was weak, couldn't feel anything, my vision was blurry then I passed out the next minute.

Before I was fully awake in the hospital, I thought I was dead and funny thing is, I thought I was on my way to Heaven. All that I could see was light, but it turned out to be the hospital light which was over my face. The nurse woke me up and when I asked her what had happened, she firstly said that I was lucky to be alive since I had lost a lot of blood.

She called Lerumo in and I thanked him for saving my life. But he had some bad news to tell me. He had spent all his savings on the hospital bills. It was a private hospital and he took me there because my situation was quite critical that if I was taken to a public hospital, I would've died since the service is always poor.

He told me that I had to pay him back all his money. I almost had a heart-attack when he showed me the bill he paid. It then reminded me of what the old prophet said about how my parents will have financial problems. That was it, the bill was three times my parent's salaries combined. I had to go home and explain to them what had happened.

I got a phone call as I was packing stuff and clothes that I'd need when I was in KZN. It was my father telling me that my mother was fired at work. Apparently she was mobilizing people for a salary increase strike. That was absolutely crap! My mother was a God fearing woman and she wasn't much of an opinion leader or a people's person. She would never do anything like that. It was just another bad thing that the old lady promised would happen. I told my dad that I was on my way home. My stress levels increased.

I got a lift to the Johannesburg bus station the following morning. But there weren't any buses that were traveling to KZN so I had to take a taxi. I knew it wasn't safe but I had no choice. I walked to the taxi rank as it wasn't far from the bus station. I found the taxi travelling to KZN and graciously, they were only waiting for one more person to fill the empty seat. And that happened to be me. Without any more waiting, the taxi drove off.

I slept right after the taxi had left the province. But a few minutes into my sleep, I felt a sudden bang on the back of the taxi and the next thing, the taxi was rolling down the road…

I then woke up in the hospital, three days later as I was told. I couldn't feel any part of my body. I couldn't even move my head to look around. It was only after a few moments of trying to make a sound that my mother realized that I was awake. We spoke about what had happened although I was struggling to speak. I asked her why I couldn't feel any part of my body and she burst into tears. After a while, she revealed that I would be fine but I am never going to see the use of my legs.

I felt an awful emotion overtaking me. I couldn't cry, not because I held the tears back. I just couldn't produce any tears. And that just showed the effect that the accident had. But my heart ached. The thought of not using my legs again tore me apart.

Nothing else mattered. I didn't care about the old woman's curses anymore. I didn't want to think about the money I owed Lerumo. I felt that my life was over.

VOICES:

PIECES OF A TRANSSEXUAL PASTOR

1

Judge Elelwani was given a second chance to live.

His family and friends were frustrated. They searched for a surgeon from South Africa to the rest of Africa and they failed to find one. His brain tumor was intense, and it worsened by the day. His wife Portia got wiry each time she laid her eyes on him. She was on the brink of giving up as she watched life slowly quitting on her husband.

''Her faith was being put to the test,''-was what her pastor suggested as the answer to all the misery that her family was going through. But doubts were slowly creeping in since she had fasted and prayed for forty days and forty nights. Still, there was no miracle or intervention of some sort. Maria, her mother in law, kept saying that her son was being punished for all his sins. His job as a judge in the court of law was quite a tough one. He was always under the scrutiny of the public for his judgments on high profile cases. No one paid attention to Maria because she was a psychiatric patient.

2

Pastor Ben couldn't fall back to sleep again as he was terrified by the nightmare he had. More frightening was seeing his wife in the nightmare, but he didn't like to think of it as a nightmare since he was receiving a message from Voices, *God's Spiritual Messenger*. He then got out of bed making sure he didn't wake his wife Kyra. Silently, he tiptoed to his prayer room. For the very first time a gash of doubts flooded his mind. It had never happened before. He wouldn't doubt what Voices was conveying to him. Every encounter with God was always an interpersonal communication, but what Voices conveyed to him that fateful early morning looked incredibly scary and he couldn't respond to it.

Pastor Ben was a transsexual and nobody knew, including his wife. He was originally from Zambia. He moved to South Africa to pursue tertiary education but that was not the only reason. From his upbringing, he felt trapped in his body, he couldn't relate with other girls and that caused a low-self-esteem in him. Matters worsened when he reached puberty. He started liking girls, and it was a taboo to be sexually attracted to members of the same sex in Zambia. Hence he moved to South Africa where he believed he would be free to be who he truly was.

In the dream that he had, God wanted him to heal Judge Elelwani. Frustrating as it was, he was eager to do it. But he couldn't connect the dots. Why would God want him to heal some strange man? And in the same dream his real sex comes up, including images of Doctors performing a 'sex-reassignment-surgery' on him. More alarming was that his wife stood at the door crying while Doctors performed the surgery. He asked Voices what was happening but Voices didn't know as Voices was just a messenger of the Most High. Voices only advised him to heal Judge Elelwani as soon as possible.

Prior to Pastor Ben's move to South Africa, he had applied to study Actuarial Sciences at Wits. He was admitted and he finished his degree in record time. When he got a job, he began saving for the sex-reassignment-surgery. It was quite expensive to get that kind of surgery done as there were few surgeons in South Africa, but from the few that were available, they were highly skilled.

Before Pastor Ben got the surgery done, Voices warned Pastor Ben about it and he didn't obey him. Voices was an intermediary. Most of the time, he was invisible but present in spirit. It was only in times of distress that Voices appeared in flesh to Pastor Ben. Their relationship started right after Pastor Ben was baptized at thirteen years old. When he heard his voice for the first time, he was startled. He thought he was going mad. But Voices knew his thoughts so he assured him that he wasn't going mad.

When Pastor Ben was going through depression and sexual frustration in his teen years, Voices was there for him. He couldn't comprehend what was happening to him as a young girl. It was all too complex for him to figure out what was happening. But Voices was his shoulder to cry on and promised him that it will all be over soon. He was there for him every step of the way. Voices did not judge him, but rather gave him comfort in God's word. Pastor Ben knew what the bible's standpoint was on homosexuality together with the laws of the country and it did not make him feel any better. That's when he thought of letting go of his religious life and escaping to another country. But he couldn't change his religion since he had spiritual gifts. And if he didn't respond to the Calling, nothing was going to be well in his life.

When he got to university, he lived in disgust. He loathed the way other guys tried to flirt with him especially when they asked him out. He wasn't attracted to any of them. He liked girls but he was still trying to find his feet and coming out would just be a disaster. All that he wanted was a lover, someone to give him a reason to wake up every day. Even though he was living in South Africa "the free land," he still wasn't entirely free.

3

He was praying, asking God to reveal why he had assigned him to heal Judge Elelwani but there wasn't any response. Such assignments were not new to him. He was only terrified by the way it was presented to him.

His wife, Kyra, walked in the prayer room. She was surprised as she could hear him from their bedroom upstairs. Pastor Ben prayed fiercely and loudly when it was fasting time, not on any other event. So Kyra thought something was wrong and when she asked him, he told her the truth, Just not all of it. He left out the part about his sex reassignment surgery and only spoke about healing a Judge that was sick. He left out the surgery part because he didn't want Kyra to know.

Kyra didn't doubt anything that she was told, she took it as it was. She didn't read too much into such situations as they involved God. She invested her energy in being the mother of the church and doing Pastor's wife duties and subsequently juggling her medical career. She was an inspiration to many girls in the church. Some people called her "Superwoman" as she was able to multitask in a fairly busy life. But those who hated her would always say that there was nothing keeping her busy as she didn't have any children.

4

Portia and her Son Phathu, were called by the hospital because Judge Elelwani was going to be taken to surgery that day. The hospital found a neurosurgeon who just happened to be around town and they pleaded her if she could help Judge Elelwani. And after lot of begging and negotiating she agreed. But she was available for that day only, therefore, they had to contact the family immediately. When they got there, all they had to do was to sign off the consent in surgery. As Portia was about to sign, Pastor Ben barged in the office and stopped her.

He grabbed the paper away from her and he tore it into pieces. This made Phathu furious! He jumped in front of Pastor Ben with clenched fists, Pastor Ben not looking horrified, he stood still and waited for what Phathu intended. As he was about to punch him, Pastor Ben began exorcising Phathu, within a second Phathu was tripped to fall down. Demons began manifesting in him, he was trembling, shaking and turning. When nurses tried to get him up, Pastor Ben told them not to as the demons would enter them.

Portia couldn't understand what was happening, she looked at Pastor Ben showing frustration, and so did the nurses. He looked at them and told them to give him a moment, without any queries they all nodded. They didn't want to end up like Phathu on the ground as it was clear that he was undergoing a certain level of pain. The demons that were manifesting in Phathu were the demons of Lust and Hate.

Phathu was married and the marriage survived only three years. He was cheating. At first, his wife forgave him, he did it again, and she warned him. After sometime, he cheated again, she pretended as if she didn't care then he started indulging into it. He became proud of it and she had enough. So she left him.

He wasn't having affairs with other women. He was having an affair with himself. Phathu was addicted to watching adult movies while pleasuring himself. He was addicted to watching other people getting it on, and doing all sorts of sexual acts to each other. He preferred pleasuring himself to intercourse with his wife. That led to their divorce.

But that demon was cast out that day. He was also possessed with the demon of hate. He hated his father, Judge Elelwani. He was never a son to him, he was treated like property. All the other children were perfect in his eyes, because they were intelligent in academics and never repeated any grades like him. Judge Elelwani loved the other three as they were ''fit'' for public exhibition. They didn't have any disease like bipolar disorder which Phathu had and in his father's eyes, it was too embarrassing. When they were at the hospital Phathu wanted to see him die, that was part of the reason he went to the hospital. But according to Pastor Ben, it was all a demon. Including the bipolar disorder.

He finally woke up. All demons cast out. Pastor Ben spoke to them and indicated that the surgery cannot be performed as Judge Elelwani was going to die if it was done. Portia could not help but ask why he thought her husband would die. Pastor Ben didn't want to talk much as he had to go home. He asked to be taken to the ward and they took him there.

When he got inside he asked to be left alone with Judge Elelwani. They all left and he began praying. He touched his head and asked for healing until Voices said that it was done! He was healed, the brain tumor was gone.

5

Portia was ecstatic about her husband's recovery although she had already threw in the towel. In her head, she had begun with burial preparations as there was no sign of recovery before Pastor Ben came. All that she had was just hope, which had ran out.

Phathu on the contrary, was trying figure out who the man that cast out demons in him and also healed his father was. When he asked his mother and the nurses, they also had the same question but it didn't matter to them since Judge Elelwani was healed.

The other family members were told the good news and they rejoiced with them. But they also had good news to share. Maria, the psychiatric patient, was also miraculously healed.

She received her healing at the same time as her son. But she was possessed with demons. When the healing took place, demons were manifesting in her. The family was confused by what was happening, they tried to calm her down but the demonic spirits gave her immense strength. When the demons had been cast out, she confessed to the family members what had been happening. Her "real self'' was caught in a cave with bees. They would sting her every time her ''physical self'' was exposed to the preaching's of God. This happened for fifteen years.

Voices was pleased with Pastor Ben He got the job done although he didn't comprehend why he had to do it. But as Pastor Ben was leaving the hospital, leaving the family to celebrate Judge Elelwani's healing, he was warned by Voices that he must prepare himself for a battle.

Circumstances were going to change, in fact, his life was going to be turned upside down. Pastor Ben interpreted it as a spiritual warfare. He wasn't moved at all since God had always given him the power to defeat Satan in many situations. But Voices warned him again. Voices knew that it wasn't just a spiritual warfare. It seemed like bloodshed, so much was going to be destroyed and a lot of people were going to be hurt. And Voices knew that it wasn't Satan that was going to attack him.

He arrived home and was stunned at the sight of an old Toyota taxi parked on his lawn. This puzzled him. He didn't have any friends that owned Vehicles of that kind, particularly a taxi that didn't have a South African registration. He thought that he knew the plate number registration, he had seen it before but couldn't reminisce exactly where. The only way to get out of that mystery was entering the house and finding out who the guest was. Before he got out off the car, he asked his driver if he had any idea of what was going on but he didn't know anything. It was shocking, a taxi parked inside the yard, on his dear lawn.

He got out of the car eager to find out who had the guts and baffling disrespect to park their 90's taxi on his green grass.

He barged into the house calling Kyra to explain what was happening. Indeed was he a pastor and it was not expected of him to be angry about small things such as parking a taxi on a lawn since to some people it was just a grass. But his lawn was special, his whole garden was very dear to him, he worked on it himself. It was a sacred place in his house.

Kyra called him to the leaving room, and he got the shock of his life! He almost fainted! He was trembling, looked as if he had seen ghosts. His worst nightmare was live, it was happening, he never thought of the reality of that day because he had cursed it, even rebuked it in prayer! But we don't always get what we want. Before his vision were his parents

6

Coup de main! Pastor Ben felt it!

He knew that was it, he had a gash feeling! He had not seen his parents in twenty years. He lied about them. He told people, including his wife, that they died of AIDS.

When Pastor Ben left Zambia to go study in South Africa, he had no intention of going back there as its constitution was against homosexuality. He didn't tell his parents anything, all that they knew was that he was going to study and he would only return home during the Christmas holiday. But he never did.

In his first year of study, Pastor Ben changed his names. He didn't want to be tracked by any of his friends or relatives. He wanted to start a new life in South Africa on a new slate. It was a bit difficult for him at first to change his identity as he was a foreigner but Voices led him and brought favour upon him. By the end of second semester, after a lot of trials and errors, he finally changed his identity, hence his parents never found him until today.

They found it difficult not only because he changed his identity but because they were poor. Searching for a missing person in South Africa was expensive. The only way to go was through a private entity and they couldn't afford that.

Kyra tried to put herself together and calmly asked Pastor Ben to sit down. He hesitated before he took a seat far from where his parents were sitting. He avoided making eye contact with anyone, he shamefully faced down knowing very well that he had been caged and there was nowhere to run to. It was confession time.

His father couldn't believe what was before his eyes. A man who was his daughter. He couldn't fathom what was happening. When he was told that his little girl was now transsexual man, he had to undergo a short educational course. Trans-sexuality didn't exist in Zambia. Not even a thought of it came to play in the mind. It was more than just a taboo. Sexuality was a one-way route, *"men get attracted to women and women get attracted to men."* Nothing other than that existed in their minds. Hence he had to be taught about sexuality when he was told that his daughter is no longer a girl.

His mother asked herself if she was dreaming, and Pastor Ben slowly looked up at her and assured her that it was real and it was happening. He confirmed that he was indeed their daughter who just went through a few changes. His mother processed the news in her head before she looked at him with great disgust. Kyra burst into tears. She felt betrayed, and thought she was an idiot and so stupid. She believed him when he said he was infertile and God didn't want him to have children of his own.

Her Indian family didn't approve of her marriage. The reasons for that were obvious. Pastor Ben was a Christian and he was black. Kyra was an Indian woman from the Islam religion. Her family strongly believed that the two didn't mix and the marriage would be cursed if they continued with it.

At that moment Kyra reminisced of what her father told her on her wedding day. He made it clear that their marriage was cursed before it even began and she would run back to him when it fell apart. She regretted not listening to him and loathed what she had become. She gave her whole life to Pastor Ben, from converting to Christianity to reducing her working hours at her medical profession just to be his wife and work for the church!

She had so much anger in her. But what troubled her was the fact that she was married to a woman. The man whom she thought was a man was actually a female at birth. When he tried to explain himself to her, she pushed him away and spat on him before she left the room.

"Sarai" murmured his father.

Pastor Ben looked away pretending not to have heard that name. His Father said it again but this time there was grief in his tone and tears rolled down his cheeks. He asked him what they have done to him that he had to put them through awful misery, and continued saying that they might not have given him everything that he wanted when he was growing up but they loved him. They tried to be the best parents but poverty always found a way to make them seem as if they do not care. As more tears dropped, he asked why he had to change himself into a man. With all the knowledge he acquired about trans-sexuality, he still didn't understand. It was difficult for him to comprehend what his daughter had become. He raised her as a girl, she behaved like a girl, and she was surrounded by women that loved her dearly. With all that information, he found it difficult to come up with a possible "reasonable" explanation of why his daughter changed her sexuality.

7

Pastor Ben explained everything in detail from the beginning. Kyra came back in while he was still telling the story. She hated being in his presence and wanted to leave but she wanted to know the whole story, so she sat down and listened.

Everything that he said to them was making sense but what puzzled them was the spiritual side of things. They didn't understand why he was blessed with a spiritual gift and how he became a Pastor. Kyra questioned him about that. They both knew that sexuality in terms of religion was a one-way street. But Pastor Ben thought differently about that. Kyra didn't care about his thoughts as she looked at what was in the bible. She knew what the scriptures in the bible said about sexuality. But the Bible does not explicitly mention anything about trans-sexuality. The closest it comes to mentioning trans-sexuality is in its condemnations of homosexuality. And Pastor Ben used that to defend himself. It didn't make any sense to his parents and Kyra. They all thought it was ridiculous and he was playing God.

Pastor Ben got angry and started interrogating them on why God was using him powerfully to change the community. Why was he blessed with the gift of healing? He had saved many lives and souls through his ministry and he never felt any guilt because God knew whom he was, he believed that God created him in that way. Yes he was a girl at birth but he didn't feel like that. He was trapped in a female's body and he wanted to escape and be what God created him to be.

Pastor Ben's father couldn't stand to listen to what he thought was nonsense. He got up and said to him that his God might be the one underground and expressed his disappointment and regretted of coming to his house. His mother stood up too and she also left the room. Before they were outside, Pastor Ben asked them how they found him. Without any hesitation, his mother said it was Kyra's father.

Pastor Ben also remembered the words that Kyra's father uttered to him on the wedding day. He had told him that his marriage wasn't going to work and he would try everything in his power to make sure that it fails. All that he needed was time. When Pastor Ben thought he was just expressing his anger since he didn't want his daughter to be married to a black man and he would soon calm down and realize that his daughter's happiness was important. But that didn't happen, Pastor Ben thought wrong. Everything was about to fall apart.

Kyra moved out the same day although Pastor Ben tried to stop her, she had already made up her mind about leaving him. She felt betrayed and stupid. She struggled to comprehend how she didn't realize all that when he told her that he cannot have children and it was a "family thing." She was a medical doctor, one of the best in the country, why didn't she ask to conduct some medical tests on him just to confirm his theory. If he was right, she could've found another way to have children. But no, she sacrificed her life and watched her child-bearing years go by without looking for a way around the circumstances.

Before she left, she made sure Pastor Ben was warned about what was coming his way. She wanted a divorce, with half of everything and she was suing him for misrepresentation.